SIX WEEKS OF WELLNESS

EDWARD FERNON

Six Weeks of Wellness

Tellwell Talent
www.tellwell.ca

ISBN
978-0-2288-8671-6 (Hardcover)
978-0-2288-8670-9 (Paperback)
978-0-2288-8701-0 (eBook)

Introduction

In 2013, I had an experience that forced me to completely rethink how I live my life. For months I had been burning the candle at both ends. I was setting up my own business, studying for my Masters, working part-time and pushing myself to the limit physically every day as I trained for the Olympics. This led me to become heavily overstimulated, sleep deprived and stressed. One day I was running in Centennial Park in Sydney and suddenly I was hit by a fatigue wall. It felt like all my energy in an instant was completely sucked out of me and I collapsed, unable to move. That moment started me on my wellness journey. Now I take pride in being able to help others in pursuit of true well-being through the Brightlands Retreat business.

Brightlands Retreat is a retreat and wellness centre focused on creating soul nurturing experiences. We strive to provide a sanctuary for you to relax, recharge and escape the noise of the world. This book was written for our many guests who have asked for a guide to help live the Brightlands way because if we want to redefine what it means to live a successful life, we need to integrate wellness into our daily lives.

When I refer to wellness, I am referring to complete health, rather than just physical health.

Wellness is about having a purpose in life, being fit and healthy, managing stress, being emotionally stable, living in a safe environment, having quality relationships, and striving for happiness. Wellness is not a static state but rather an active pursuit that forms part of your life. It is about having responsibility for our choices and behaviours that lead towards an optimal state of wellbeing.

Many people find that stress and a busy lifestyle make it difficult to focus on wellness. We often hear people say that they're "too busy" but really, they just haven't developed healthy habits. 6 weeks of Wellness is all about implementing small healthy habits that can lead to large changes in your life.

To help you along your wellness journey, I have compiled six weeks' worth of exercises and questions, with each week focusing on one area of wellness found in the Brightlands Wellness Wheel. There are four internal drivers of wellness being: purpose, growth, mind and body and two external drivers being environment and community. Together they combine to create a holistic guide to wellness.

At the end of 6 weeks, reflect on everything you've done. What tips did you enjoy and get benefit from? What would you like to continue doing? Following these tips only once will not form a lasting habit. The key is to reflect and select a few activities and commit to doing them daily. As Tony Robbins says, "It's not what we do once in a while that shapes our lives. It's what we do consistently."

My wish for you is that you find your own unique combination of wellness methods and turn them into habits so that they provide you with sustained energy and sense of purpose, ready to conquer life's challenges.

COMMUNITY
MIND
GROWTH
PURPOSE
BODY
ENVIROMENT

Brightlands Wellness Wheel

Purpose: Purpose is all about what gives life meaning. Purpose drives life's decisions, habits, behaviours, goals and direction.

Growth: Growth is about challenging ourselves to be the best person we can possibly be. It involves being willing to move outside our comfort zone and engaging the world through learning and problem-solving.

Mind: Tapping into our subconscious mind is the key to realising our unlimited potential. It also involves improving our mental health and harnessing our emotions.

Body: Being physically fit and healthy.

Environment: We not only need to consider the natural environment but also what we expose ourselves to.

Community: Connecting and engaging with others and making a positive impact on those around us.

Week 1: Purpose

A meaningful life is the basis for good health and wellbeing. Purpose is about living with passion, doing meaningful work towards a meaningful goal, where we feel a part of something greater than ourselves often in the service of others.

We are at our best when we dedicate ourselves to something greater than ourselves. The best place to start is to consider ones *ikigai*, which is the age-old Japanese ideology of finding joy in life through purpose. Your ikigai is what gets you up every morning and keeps you going. We find our ikigai within the overlap of these four main qualities: what you love, what you are good at, what the world needs and what you can be paid for. Once you understand your ikigai, your purpose will become clearer.

Day 1: What brings you joy?

In the town of Kyotango in Japan there are three times more residents over the age of 100 compared to the average of the rest of the country. When scientists researched the residents they found exceptionally high figures of DHEA, a steroid hormone secreted by the adrenal glands. Of all the people with high figures of DHEA they found one single thing they all had in common: they had a hobby they practiced every day that they really enjoyed.

In Plato's Apology Socrates defines his life's mission as awakening the Athenians to the supreme importance of attending to their souls. This timeless plea asks us to connect with ourselves and understand what brings us joy.

Questions:

What do you love doing?

What would you do if you knew you wouldn't fail?

Day 2: Identify your strengths?

Strengths are a combination of skills, knowledge and talent. Understanding your strengths is important in helping you maximise your potential. If you want to delve deeper than the questions below you can undertake the Gallup Clifton Strengths Assessment or the VIA Character Strengths Survey.

Questions:

What are you good at?

What comes easy to you?

What do others say your strength are?

What do others ask advice on?

Day 3: What does the world need?

According to future trends what could you imagine doing that taps into your gifts, talents, strengths and passions. A critical consideration here is picturing the next 4, 10 and 20 years.

Questions:

What could I offer the world?

What technological or market trends are affecting my industry or type of work?

Will your work still be valuable in 5, 10, 20 years time?

Day 4: What can you be paid for?

"You don't get paid for the hour. You get paid for the value you bring to the hour." Jim Rohn

It isn't enough to only consider joy, passion and what the world needs as we also need to be able to make ends meet for ourselves and our families. Considering what we can be paid for is important to ensure what we commit ourselves to is viable in the long term.

Questions:

Is there anyone else doing what you want to do? What do they get paid?

What creative ways could you monetise this?

What partnerships or sponsorships could assist you on the journey?

Day 5: Dream Book

Keeping in mind the questions answered in the previous four days it is now time to identify your own ikigai and create a dream book. This goes beyond simply writing down your goals. A dream book is a book that is private for the individual and includes all goals, dreams, and aspirations.

Activity:

Buy a quality leather bound book with plain paper and fill it with all your hopes and dreams. The more detail with pictures and colour the better so feel free to get creative.

Day 6: Visualise your ideal day

The main benefit of visualisation is that it helps you get more of what you want. When you vividly imagine achieving your goals you trigger your subconscious mind, which will help you reach your goals faster and more effortlessly. The subconscious brain is a goal seeking machine and doesn't know the difference between real and imaginary experiences so when you visualise what you want it will guide you to that reality.

Activity:

Close your eyes, take three deep breath and then completely relax. It may help to slowly count down from 10. Once you are relaxed think of something you want to achieve or an experience you want to have. What can you see? What are the smells around you? What people are with you? What noise can you hear? And most importantly how does it make you feel? What emotions rise to the surface when you've achieved this goal? Who do you want to share it with?

Day 7: Write your personal memoir

"The only calibration that counts is how much heart people invest, how much they ignore their fears of being hurt or caught out or humiliated. And the only thing people regret is that they didn't live boldly enough, that they didn't invest enough heart, didn't love enough. Nothing else really counts at all."

Ted Hughes

A memoir is a summary of what your life is about. Your defining moments and impactful experiences. Writing our memoir and reflecting on the past helps us to shape the present and future.

Activity:

Write your own memoir focusing not on what you did but rather what kind of life you lived.

Week 2: Growth

"In this world you're either growing or you're dying, so get in motion and grow." Lou Holtz.

Growth is about challenging ourselves to be the best person we can possibly be. It involves staying in a continuous state of learning which will make you healthier, happier, more interesting and more valuable. The questions and activities for this week will help guide you towards growth in your life.

Day 8: Establish a morning routine

As soon as we wake up our minds are often flooded with all the things that we need to do. This can feel so overwhelming that you can end up wasting time. A morning routine means you perform the same basic tasks in the same order every day. There are numerous benefits to a morning routine but the leading benefit is the ability to get in the right frame of mind to help us prepare for the day ahead. If you want an extra energy boost, include a high-intensity workout, meditation, or a cold shower in your morning routine

Question:

What does a great start to the day look like for you?

How do you make this happen for yourself?

What habits do you have that are holding you back?

What habits are adding value to your life?

Day 9: What are three things I MUST do today to help turn my dream into reality?

These are non-negotiable must do things that you must commit to no matter how you feel. By completing these tasks day in and day out not only do you get closer to your goals but you also build resilience and determination. These are often small tasks but day after day they lead to big changes.

Activity:

Write down the three most important tasks that need to be completed today. Prioritise these tasks first before you start anything else in your day.

Day 10: Time-blocking

A 40 hour time-blocked work week, I estimate, produces the same amount of output as a 60+ hour work week pursued without structure."
Cal Newport, Author of Deep Work

We are constantly bombarded in our modern world with distractions and noise. The reality is if you don't control your schedule, it will control you. Time blocking is one of the most effective productivity strategies as it helps us prioritise what's important, keeps us focused and restores energy throughout the day. Time blocking is a time management method that asks you to divide your day into blocks of time. Each block is dedicated to a specific task. Instead of keeping an open-ended to-do list of things, you start each day with a concrete schedule that lays out what you'll work on and when.

Most people start their workdays with their emails and then they slowly work through the rest of their tasks from easiest to hardest. The issue with opening your email is that it prioritises other people's tasks before your own and we can get easily side-tracked. We have the most energy and creativity in the morning so we should be focused on the most difficult and creative tasks first.

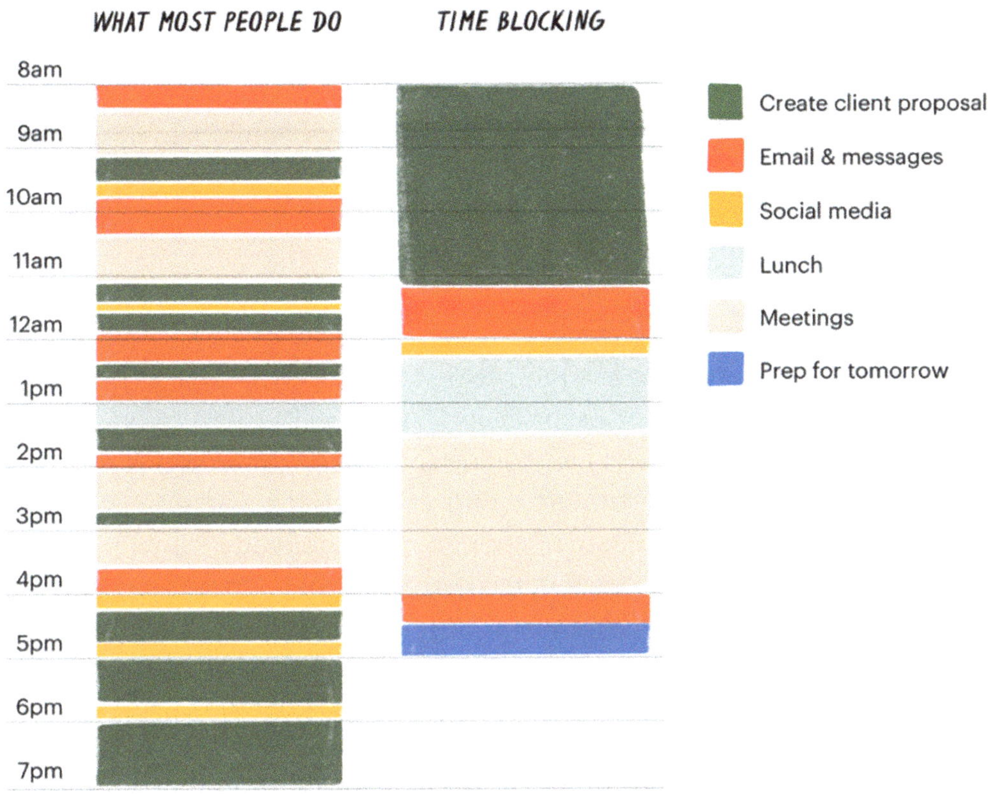

Source: Jayson DeMers: How to Use Time Blocking for Productivity: 18 Practical Ways

Activity:

Break your day up into 50-minute increments. At the end of the 50 minutes give yourself a ten-minute break to walk around, go to the bathroom and have a drink. Prioritise the most important and creative tasks first and the tasks that need less brain power later in the day. Turn off email notifications and other distractions. Give yourself two times during the day in the morning and afternoon that you respond to emails.

Day 11: Gripe Journaling

Many people use journaling to helps clear their mind and get perspective on what's important. Gripe journaling specifically focuses on what is upsetting and worrying you as once these issues are on paper, they can be released and help resolve the tension caused by holding on.

Activity:

Write down everything that is worrying or annoying you. Once you have your list imagine that a friend has just given you this list. What is one piece of advice you would give your friend to find a solution for each issue. It may help to ask yourself:

- What is the worst thing that can happen?
- Can I handle the worst-case scenario?
- Can I improve on the worst-case scenario?

Day 12: Find a role model, mentor or coach

"Surround yourself with only those that lift you higher." Oprah Winfrey

Role models and mentors are not only a source of inspiration they also provide us with a road map of how to achieve our goals. Role models have often developed strategies and attitudes that lead to success, that you can apply to your own life. They have overcome similar obstacles and failures that you can learn from meaning you don't need to reinvent the wheel.

Question:

Name three people who have already achieved what you want to achieve or who are further along the path? Send them a letter or email and tell them why you admire them and that you'd like to connect.

Day 13: Read

Reading helps improve focus, concentration, vocabulary, memory but also and most importantly it provides us with new perspectives and ideas.

Activity:

Make a list of the books you want to read in priority order and then allocate time in your day for reading them.

Day 14: Try a new skill or course

Having a hobby may help reduce stress and help foster social ties as well as making you more efficient at managing your time. Opening yourself to something new encourages a growth mindset, which allows you to build a curiosity about the world.

Activity:

Write a list of all the things you'd like to do that you haven't done before. Then find a teacher or class where you can try. Make a commitment to attending the class.

Week 3: Mind

There are thousands of research papers that indicate that we really can increase happiness by purposefully changing our thinking patterns. The following activities this week help to nourish the mind and provide the tools to improve your mental health.

Day 15: Gratitude

"Be content with what you have, rejoice in the way things are. When you realise there is nothing lacking, the whole world belongs to you." Lao Tzu

"The root of you is gratefulness. It is not joy that makes us grateful; it is gratitude that makes us joyful." Br. David Steindl-Rast

Gratitude involves thinking about the positive things in your life and how thankful you are for them. Expressing gratitude is one of the leading indicators of happiness and helps to reduce stress, improves self-esteem and improves the quality of your relationships.

Activity:

Try the ten-finger gratitude exercise. List ten events or things that you are truly grateful for. It could be something that someone did for you or a special event or moment.

How did it make you feel?

How is your life richer for these events or moments?

Day 16: Affirmations

We can often be our own worst enemy letting negativity foster in our head. What we say to ourselves has a huge impact on our self-esteem and how we live our life. People often spend too much time focusing on what they don't want rather than what they do want. Positive self-talk reverses this state by helping to reduces stress, increase confidence and allowing us to adopt a healthier lifestyle.

Activity:

Create three mantra's that you can repeat on a daily basis. Here are some suggestions:

- I am happy, healthy, wealthy and wise.
- I am capable and confident.
- I am a champion.
- No matter how hard things are I'm going to make it.
- I'm doing the best I can.
- Every day I am getting better and better at.....
- I feel energetic and alive.
- My life is unfolding beautifully.
- I love challenges and what I learn from overcoming them.

Day 17: Float Tank

The main benefit of using a sensory deprivation tank is to ease anxiety and muscle tension. The water temperature should be set to body temperature and in combination with the buoyancy allows for a complete feeling of relaxation. Many guests at Brightlands Retreat have commented that this is what it must feel like being back in the womb. Floating in a tank can also relieve migraines and provide stress relief and detoxification since Epsom salts are high in magnesium, which can remove harmful substances such as free radicals from your body.

Activity:

Try 60 mins in a float tank

Day 18: Create your war chest

When times get tough having a variety of resources you can draw on helps restore your mood and will bring a greater sense of confidence into the present moment.

Activity:

- Write down a list of all your life achievements?
- What are three times you have faced a major challenge and have managed to overcome the situation?
- What are the three funniest things that have ever happened to you?
- Who is the one person that always makes you happy in their presence?
- What are ten of your favourite photos?
- Where is your happy place?

Day 19: Meditation

There are many different types of meditation but essentially it is about taking time to connect with your inner self. Meditation is a powerful tool to deal with stress and anxiety and allows us to take back control and focus on achieving our goals.

Activity:

Try this simple meditation practice:

1) Take a seat or lie down in a place that is quiet and where you will not be disturbed.
2) Undertake a body scan from your toes all the way to the top of your head. As you slowly focus on each part of your body notice if there is any tension there. Squeeze each individual muscle for 2-3 seconds and then release.
3) Focus on your breathing- inhale for 4 seconds, hold for 4 seconds and exhale for 4 seconds then start again.
4) Inevitably, your attention will wander when meditating. When you notice this happening simply return your attention to your breathing. Don't judge yourself or obsess over the content of the thoughts.

Day 20: Learn to Reset

"Everything can be taken from a man but one thing: the last of the human freedoms—to choose one's attitude in any given set of circumstances, to choose one's own way." Viktor E. Frankl, Man's Search for Meaning

Learning to reset and recalibrate from set-backs quickly is one of the leading traits of highly successful sportspeople. When you lose a point in fencing or tennis or hit a bad shot in golf you need to quickly let go of the negative emotion and reset for the next point or shot. The same applies to when you are faced with anger, fear and resentment. We always justify why we are angry and why something should or should not have happened. You can be right in your justification, but if you want to move out of these emotions you need to be able to reset and control your attitude. The quicker you can reset the better for your mind and body as the longer you stay in that negative space the more your body becomes paralysed with cortisol.

Activity:

The next time you feel a negative emotion overtake you, quickly start a stopwatch then take three deep breaths and say to yourself "I can handle this situation and I am choosing to respond calmly."

When you are feeling like you have calmed down and your heart rate is back to normal then stop the watch. Depending on the incident initially it could take a long time to completely calm down. However, the next time try it again and see how long it takes. Soon starting the watch will become a trigger to reset and you will notice the time coming down.

Day 21: Mindfulness

To fully experience the world, we first need to be able to free ourselves from the distractions that steal our attention, such as dwelling on the past and worrying about the future. Mindfulness is living in the now. When we are mindful we become aware that we are awake and we learn to observe what is around us without judgment. One of the greatest benefits of being mindful is to learn to give our full attention to another person either listening to them or responding thoughtfully without focussing on ourselves.

Activity:

Close your eyes and focus on your breathing and be aware of your surroundings? What can you smell, taste, hear and see? Notice the weather, the leaves on trees the colours of the sky as well as those people who surround us.

Week 4: Body

Our bodies are vessels for our life on this earth and, as such, are our greatest gift, yet too many of us take our bodies for granted.

Day 22: Sleep

Of all the habits to improve wellbeing, sleep tops the list. The report undertaken by Deloitte Access Economics and commissioned by the Sleep Health Foundation found that inadequate sleep is highly prevalent in Australia with an estimated 39.8% of Australian adults experiencing some form of inadequate sleep. Lack of sleep leads to poor concentration, negative thinking, reduced impulse control, reduced emotional intelligence and a lack of empathy.

Activity:

- Use flight mode on all devices while sleeping
- Avoid caffeine in the afternoon
- Have an alarm to go to bed rather than wake up
- Try to go to bed and get up at the same time each day
- Remove all devices eg. mobile phone and lap top at least an hour before bed
- Try a short nap during the day
- Schedule time on the weekend for a sleep in or nap.

Day 23: Drink more water

This one is a no-brainer. Drinking water is good for you, especially if you're replacing sugary drinks. Increasing your water intake helps flush out your system leading to improved physical performance, energy levels and weight loss.

Activity:

Buy 3x 1L water bottles and put each in a location where you spend time each day. For example put one next to your bed, one in the car and one on your desk. When you pass the bottles during the day take a sip. Your goal is to finish the 3 litres in the day. If you don't finish it all that's ok just keep track of how much is left.

Day 24: Breathe

Taking moments in the day to stop and take some deep breaths is a great way to reset. It also helps to decrease stress, improves energy, improves clarity of decision making as well as stimulating the lymphatic system, which detoxifies the body.

Activity:

Take three moments during the day where you stop and breathe. Make sure you breathe deep into your stomach rather than your chest. There are two strategies below:

Wim Hof breathing: 25 fast deep belly breaths then a long hold and repeat 3 times.

Or

Box breathing: Inhale for 4 seconds hold for 4 seconds, then exhale for 4 second then repeat.

Day 25: Join the slow food movement

The slow food movement launched in Italy in 1989 to push back against the spread of fast food. It involves limiting any processed foods.

Activity:

Eating plenty of foods that are high in fibre such as oats, lentils, beans, onion, fruits and vegetables as well as fermented foods like yoghurt are all great for gut health.

Eating one or more servings of fatty fish per week such as salmon has been shown to provide protection against a wide range of cancers, as well as improving your mood.

Day 26: Get walking

The University of Essex researchers found that 94% of those who took part in walking, running or cycling saw mental health benefits. University of Illinois researchers showed that walking three times per week for 40 minutes helped combat the effects of ageing, increased brain connectivity and cognitive performance. In addition, walking is an easy activity to do with a companion, so can combine both social and physical benefits.

Activity:

- Take the stairs rather than the lift.
- Instead of having a meeting in a coffee shop you could take the meeting while walking.
- Take phone calls while walking.

Day 27: Cold Shower

"If we always choose comfort we never learn the deepest capabilities of our mind or body."
Wim Hof

"Today I'll choose courage over comfort."
Brené Brown

There is always something, every single day, that requires more courage than comfort. In our modern world our physical environments are very comfortable, and we rarely put our bodies through stress. Cold showers strengthen the ability to adapt to stress and when taken regularly boosts our circulatory system. This can lead to a strengthened immune system, increased energy levels and alertness and relieve symptoms of depression. Cold showers are also a fantastic way to build resilience.

Activity:

At the end of your shower each day try turning off the hot tap and leaving it completely cold. At first start with 30 seconds and then slowly build to 2-3 minutes. This is not enjoyable but it does get easier with time and the benefits compound so stick with it. If you want to take this exercise to the next step then try an ice bath for two minutes. If you would like more information then research the Wim Hof method.

Day 28: Cut the booze

A beer or glass of wine at the end of the day might bring about calm but in excess can actually do more harm than good. Alcohol is a depressant, meaning it can disrupt brain function and affect thoughts and behaviours.

Activity:

Drinking often becomes a habit so instead of reaching for a beer or wine at the end of the day try switching to a low or no alcohol substitute or your favourite tea.

Week 5: Community

Community refers to connecting and engaging with others and making a positive impact on those around us. This doesn't just include our relationships with family and friends but also includes how we treat strangers. People need people and our social networks provide significant health benefits.

People who are more socially connected to family, friends, or their community are happier, physically healthier and live longer, with fewer mental health problems than people who are less well connected" Dr Waldinger, Harvard University.

The importance of community to overall wellbeing cannot be underestimated. The Italian Roseto community in Pennsylvania between 1954 to 1961 is a perfect example of the benefits of community. The men in this community had high smoking and drinking rates, poor diets and worked in slate mines, where they were exposed to gases and dust, however there were nearly no heart attacks compared to neighbouring towns. Stewart Wolf, then head of Medicine of the University of Oklahoma in 1961, attributed the lower heart disease rate to lower stress. "The community was very cohesive. There was no keeping up with the Joneses.

Houses were very close together, and everyone lived more or less alike. Elders were revered and incorporated into community life." As the Roseto community shed their Italian social structure and became more Americanised in the years following, heart disease rates increased, becoming similar to those of neighbouring towns.

Day 29: Random Act of Kindness

"Kindness is the language that the deaf can hear and the blind can see." Mark Twain

Try doing something nice for a stranger with no strings attached. These acts may be large or small yet the effects can be profound to both the recipient and the giver.

Activity:

- Pay someone a genuine compliment.
- Buy a coffee and have a conversation with someone sitting alone at a coffee shop.
- Is there someone lonely in your street you could pay a visit to or maybe drop off a small gift?
- Provide a helping hand to someone in need.
- Try making eye contact and smiling at a stranger.

Day 30: Who is in your circle?

Some people draw a small circle only around themselves. Others draw a circle that can fit their family and friends, and then others draw a circle that encompasses everyone they come in contact with. Be mindful of your circle and your impact on others. It is important to ensure that our circles are filled with positive people that boost our energy.

Questions:

Who are the positive and negative people in your social network?

Who boosts your energy and who drains it?

Day 31: Volunteer

You may know that volunteering is good for your community, but it also has profound benefits to the those who participate in these activities. Studies show that volunteering helps reduce depression, promotes healthy blood pressure, reduces stress and supports longevity.

Activity:

- Find a cause that you are passionate about and then find a charity dealing with that issue that you could volunteer with.
- Volunteer to work at a soup kitchen.
- Spend an hour at a retirement home hearing the stories of the residents.

Day 32: Book a holiday with friends or family

Having a memorable shared experience is a great way to boost connection. This could be a weekend away or an extended overseas trip. The more the trip takes you outside your comfort zone and challenges you in a different but enjoyable way the more likely you are to grow as a person and build a connection with your travel partner or friend.

Activity:

- Write a bucket list of places you would like to visit and the experiences you would like to have.
- Have you ever considered visiting a country well off the beaten track? A place like Mongolia, Kenya or Bangladesh?

Day 33: Write a letter to someone you love

We often take for granted those that are closest and dearest to us. It is often difficult to share with them how we really feel. Writing a letter is a great way to express how much they mean to you and how grateful you are to have them in your life.

Activity:

Write a letter to someone you love addressing this person directly. Describe in specific terms what this person did and how this person has affected your life. Try to be as specific as possible. Tell them what you are doing in your life now and how their actions made an impact on you. When you are done post the letter or even better arrange to meet the person to give it to them in person.

Day 34: Organise a dinner

Quality food and good company -is there anything better? This is a great way to expand your social network as well as build connections among your friends.

Activity:

Find a date four to six weeks in the future and send out emails inviting your close friends or family to a dinner. The meal can be at a restaurant or at your home. Then savour the enjoyment you feel surrounded by people you enjoy spending time with.

Day 35: Build Rapport

Rapport is vital to meaningful relationships and describes a feeling of being 'in sync' with the other person. The activity below is provided from Dale Carnegie in his book 'how to win friends and influence people.'

Activity:

When talking to another person try to:

1) Become genuinely interested in the other person.
2) Smile.
3) Remember the person's name and use it often.
4) Encourage the person to talk about themselves and be a good listener.
5) Talk in terms of the other person's interests.
6) Make the other person feel important - and do it sincerely.

Week 6: Environment

The Global Wellness Institute outlines that “*our homes, communities and surrounding environment directly affect our daily behaviours and lifestyles, and together these determine up to 80-90% of our health outcomes.*”

“Your diet is not only what you eat, it’s what you watch, what you listen to, what you read, the people you hang around. Be mindful of the things you put in your body, emotionally, spiritually, and physically.” Wellness Mantra

Environment not only takes into account the natural environment but also what we expose ourselves to.

Day 36: Get a dose of negative Ions

Negative ions are oxygen atoms with extra negatively charged electrons. These ions are odourless, tasteless, and invisible molecules that we inhale in abundance in certain environments. Once they reach our bloodstream, negative ions are believed to produce biochemical reactions that increase levels of the mood chemical serotonin, helping to alleviate depression, relieve stress and boost our energy. One of the leading sources of positive negative ions is the beach and ocean as well as waterfalls, forests and mountains.

Activity:

- Spend some time walking on the beach or through forests or bush trails.
- Try to maintain silence as you walk and it will turn into a walking meditation as well as a well-being activity.

Day 37: Grounding

Grounding or earthing is the practice of reconnecting the human body to the earth through direct skin contact with the surface of the Earth, such as with bare feet or hands. Modern lifestyle has disconnected humans from the electrons naturally present in the ground which could contribute to increased inflammation, poor sleep and chronic pain.

Activity:

- Take a walk without shoes.
- ·Lie outside on the grass.

Day 38: Improve your home environment

The idea is to create a sanctuary from the world and a place where you can rest and recuperate as well as share with others.

Activity:

- Keep your place well ventilated and where possible allow the sun to shine in.
- Keep your environment clutter free especially in your living areas and bedroom.
- Install block out curtains in your bedroom to limit light in.
- Our bedrooms are often too warm for sleep. According to the sleep foundation the best bedroom temperature is approximately 18.3 degrees Celsius. This may vary by a few degrees from person to person, but most doctors recommend keeping the thermostat set between 15.6 to 19.4 degrees celsius for the most comfortable sleep.
- Download a sleep App and try using white noise.

Day 39: Take a break from social media

Many people don't realise that they are addicted to social media. While it can bring you good things studies show that social media may lead to anxiety, low self-esteem and social isolation.

The constant need to check your phone or see what your friends are doing can lead to social comparison and a sense of not being as good as others or missing out on what others are doing.

Activity:

- Take 1-2 days off social media per week

Day 40: Unsubscribe from unnecessary emails

Most people spend far too much time during the day dealing with emails. You don't need any more clutter in your life.

Activity:

Take an hour or two today and unsubscribe from all of those marketing emails that you don't read anyway.

Day 41: Spend time with an animal

> *"I've often said, there is nothing better for the inside of the man, than the outside of the horse." Ronald Reagan, paraphrasing Winston Churchill*
>
> *"The best therapist has fur and four legs." Goldenstars CC*
>
> *Animals can offer an extraordinary amount of emotional support and health benefits. Owning an animal can increase opportunities to exercise, get outside and socialise. According to a 2009 study published in the journal of vascular and interventional neurology cat owners are 30% less likely to have a heart attack and 40% less likely to have a stroke. Pets can also help manage loneliness and depression by giving us companionship.*

Activity:

- Find time to take a dog for a walk.
- Try equine therapy.
- Take time to pat a dog or cat

Day 42: Create a music and video playlist

Music & videos are fantastic mood boosters and great resources when you need to get into a specific mental state to help you perform. It can also have a calming affect when you are feeling emotional.

Activity:

- Create three music playlists. The first is a list of songs that help calm you down, the second paylist should motivate you and the third are your all-time favourites. Next time you get frustrated, worried or stressed try spending some time listening to playlist one. If you have an important presentation at work or moment that requires you to perform at your absolute best try listening to playlist 2. If you are feeling lonely or down try playlist 3 to help ground you and remind you of what's important.
- Save 5-10 videos on your phone that help motivate or inspire you. This might be a scene from a movie or an inspirational Youtube video. If these are readily available, it will help quickly transition you into the right mood.

FROM THE OLYMPICS TO FATIGUE AND BACK AGAIN

Edward Fernon is no stranger to success. The Olympian turned wellness advocate lives by one mantra – 'to excel in life's adventure.' After suffering from fatigue and burnout following the London 2012 Olympics, Ed has worked hard to balance his drive for success with his wellbeing which led him to starting his own wellness brand, Brightlands.

Ed's Story

Ed grew up in Sydney but for as long as he can remember he had a love of horses. Each school holidays he would visit a farm where his mother grew up near Wagga Wagga and spend time riding. Following school, Ed worked as a Jackaroo in outback Queensland, and then commenced a Bachelor of Commerce degree at Sydney University. It was at University, aged 19 that Ed took up the sport of Modern Pentathlon. He had never picked up a pistol or fencing sword and was a terrible swimmer, but after four years of intensive training he qualified and then went on to compete at the 2012 London Olympic Games as Australia's only male representative in the sport.

Following the Olympics in 2012, Edward completed a five-week-long, 1100km solo horse trek, following the legend of the first Melbourne Cup winner Archer, from Braidwood over the Snowy Mountains to Melbourne. The ride raised over $55,000 for the Black Dog Institute as well as awareness of depression in rural areas.

In 2013, Ed had an experience that forced him to completely rethink how he lived his life. For months he had been burning the candle at both ends. He was setting up his own business, studying for his Masters, working part-time and pushing himself to the limit physically every day, training for five sports. This led him to become heavily overstimulated, sleep deprived and stressed. His mentality at the time: "more is better", was not serving his mental or physical health. Running around Centennial Park in Sydney one day, Ed was hit with an overwhelming feeling, like all the energy in his body had suddenly been sucked out of him – and he collapsed, unable to move. Little did he know at the time, this was exactly what Ed needed to begin his true wellness journey, that eventually led the establishment of the Brightlands Group – so that he could help others in the pursuit of their own well-being.

After a few years of committing, rather, surrendering, to a life of wellness, in 2016, Ed embarked on a three-week expedition to summit Mount Aconcagua, the second highest of the world's seven summits and highest mountain in the Southern Hemisphere. After battling terrible weather and altitude sickness, Ed became the only member of his expedition to reach the summit.

To follow this physical and mental feat, in 2017, Ed competed in the Mongol Derby, the longest and toughest horse race in the world. The race spans 1000km across the Mongolian steppe and requires each competitor to ride 28 semi-wild Mongolian horses. Most years, only half of the competitors finish the race. Ed not only finished the race, but also won, setting a new race record in the process.

Following four years of retirement in August 2019, Ed made the decision to try to qualify for his second Olympics. He had a short intensive 12-week training program and was successful in winning the Oceania qualification spot for Tokyo 2020 in Wuhan, China in November 2019. From there he went on to compete at the Tokyo Olympic Games.

Ed's successes occur not only on horseback, but on solid ground. Ed began his property development business with an initial $5,000 investment and has gone from strength to strength and now has an impressive property portfolio and development pipeline with projects in three states of Australia centred around health and wellness.

Ed is married to Philippa and they have three boys, Xavier, Lachlan and Toby. Ed owns multiple businesses focused on wellness and improving community. This includes Brightlands Retreat which offers retreats and wellness packages, Brightlands Property fund which invests and develops residential wellness communities, and Belong Technology which is a leading community management App. Ed's passion and commitment to living and spreading wellness to Australians was born out of his own personal experiences – he found a way to overcome fatigue, and he knows that living a life of wellness works.

Ed knows that the key to success is in how you manage your drive and determination. He knows first-hand the management of your mental health and wellbeing is paramount to your success in all fields and areas of life and he continues to find ways to help others on their own wellness journey.

CPSIA information can be obtained
at www.ICGtesting.com
Printed in the USA
LVHW071552161222
735371LV00013B/1148